The Beatles
PIANO SOLOS

W9-BKG-047

ISBN 978-0-7935-4817-0

HAL•LEONARD®
CORPORATION

7777 W. BLUEMOUND RD. P.O. BOX 13819 MILWAUKEE, WI 53213

Visit Hal Leonard Online at
www.halleonard.com

ALL MY LOVING

Words and Music by JOHN LENNON
and PAUL McCARTNEY

Moderately

mf

With pedal

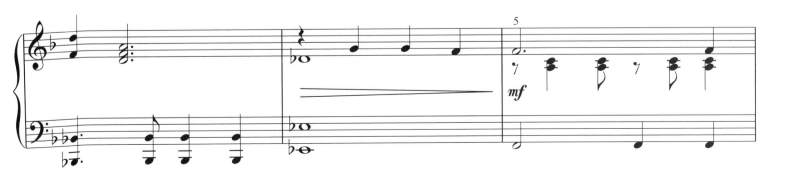

ALL YOU NEED IS LOVE

Words and Music by JOHN LENNON
and PAUL McCARTNEY

Moderately

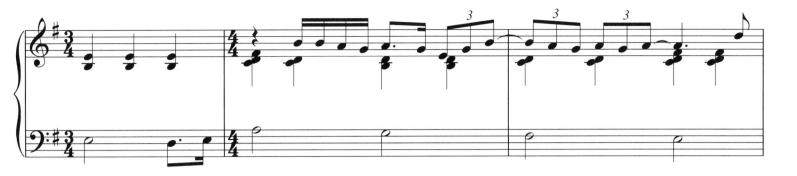

To Coda ⊕

CODA

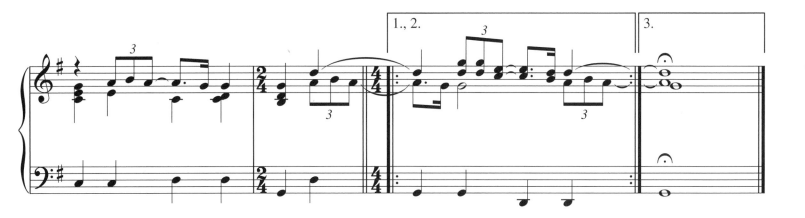

AND I LOVE HER

Words and Music by JOHN LENNON
and PAUL McCARTNEY

Moderately

mf

With pedal

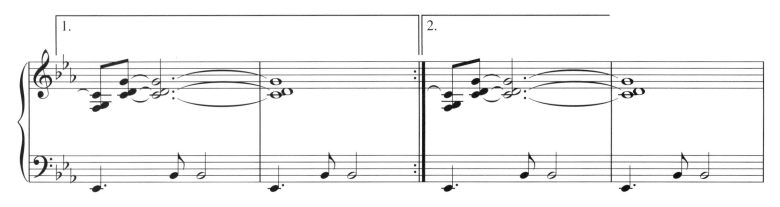

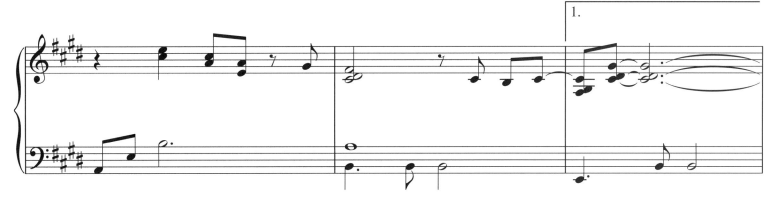

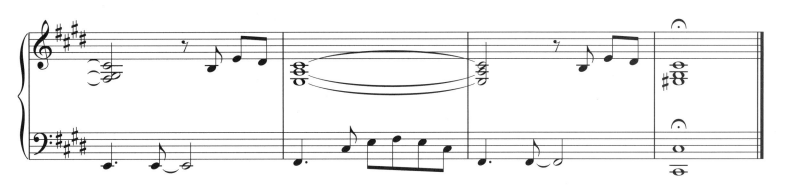

CAN'T BUY ME LOVE

Words and Music by JOHN LENNON
and PAUL McCARTNEY

Bright Shuffle

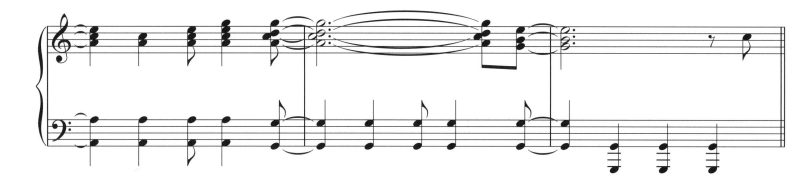

8vb

ELEANOR RIGBY

Words and Music by JOHN LENNON
and PAUL McCARTNEY

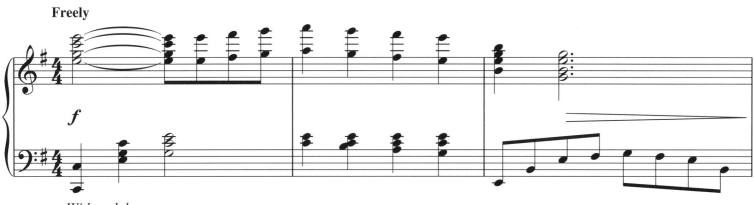

Moderately, with a steady beat

THE FOOL ON THE HILL

Words and Music by JOHN LENNON
and PAUL McCARTNEY

Moderately

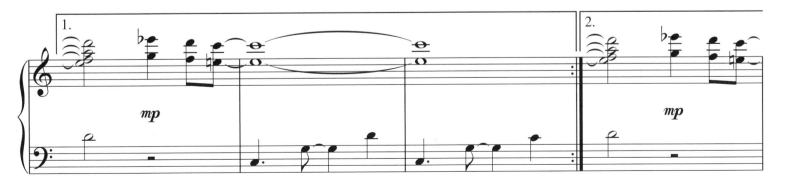

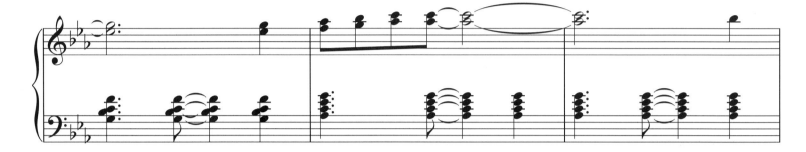

GOLDEN SLUMBERS

Words and Music by JOHN LENNON
and PAUL McCARTNEY

Moderately

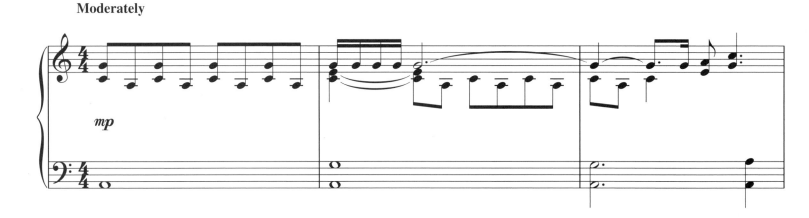

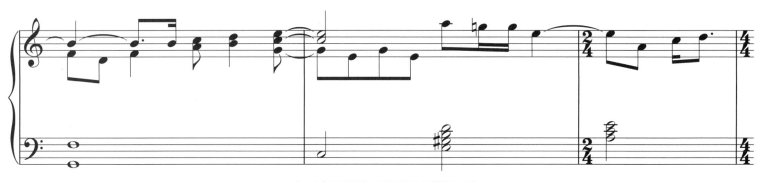

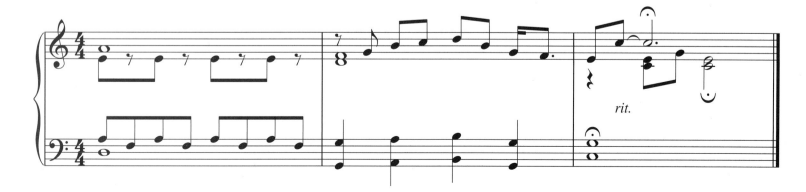

GOOD DAY SUNSHINE

Words and Music by JOHN LENNON
and PAUL McCARTNEY

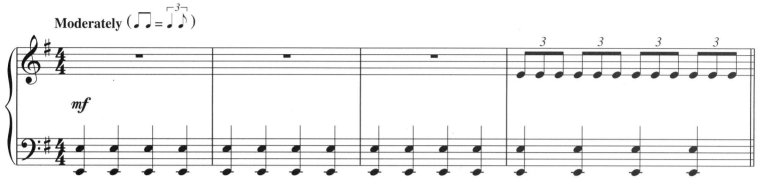

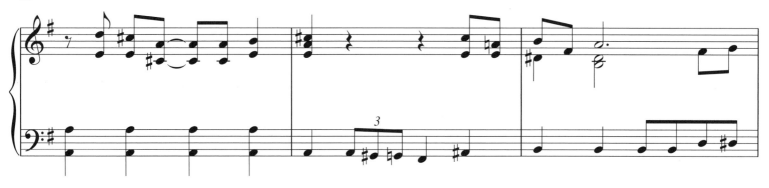

To Coda ⊕

D.S. al Coda

CODA

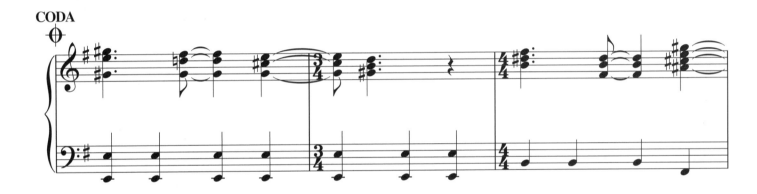

GOOD NIGHT

Words and Music by JOHN LENNON
and PAUL McCARTNEY

Slowly and tenderly

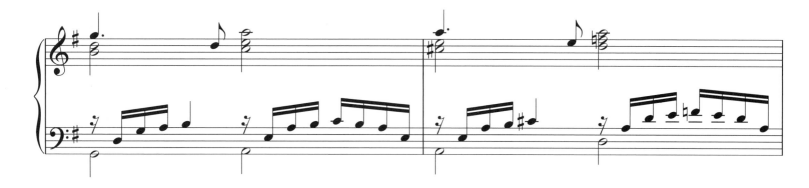

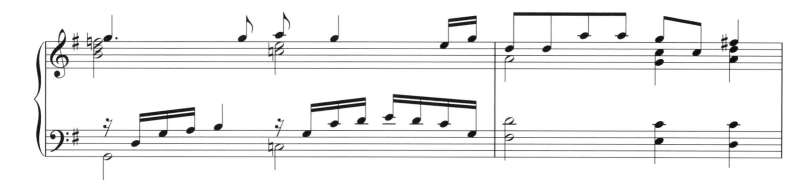

rit.

HELLO, GOODBYE

Words and Music by JOHN LENNON
and PAUL McCARTNEY

Moderately

HERE, THERE AND EVERYWHERE

Words and Music by JOHN LENNON
and PAUL McCARTNEY

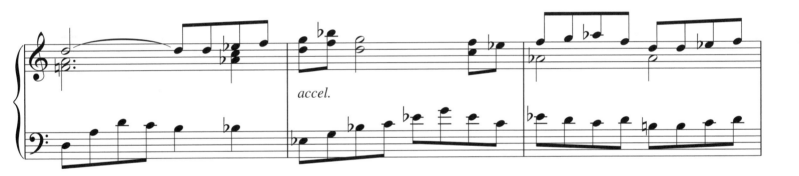

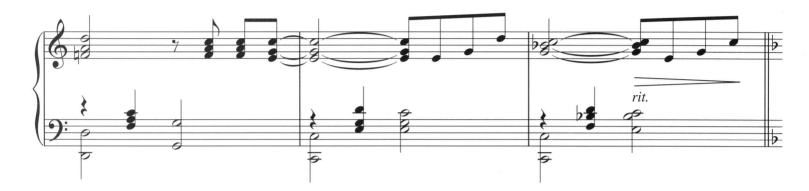

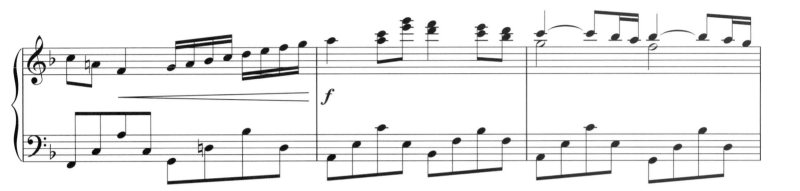

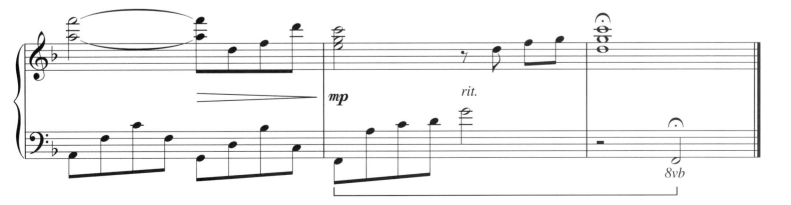

HEY JUDE

Words and Music by JOHN LENNON
and PAUL McCARTNEY

Moderately slow

IF I FELL

Words and Music by JOHN LENNON
and PAUL McCARTNEY

IN MY LIFE

Words and Music by JOHN LENNON and PAUL McCARTNEY

Moderately

mf

With pedal

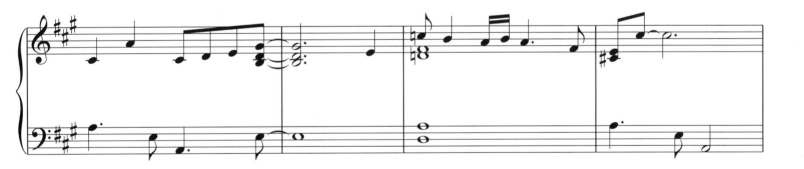

LADY MADONNA

Words and Music by JOHN LENNON
and PAUL McCARTNEY

Brightly, with a beat

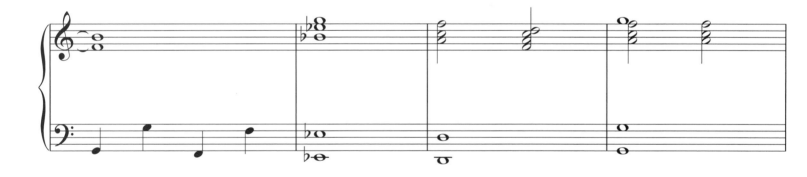

LET IT BE

Words and Music by JOHN LENNON
and PAUL McCARTNEY

Slowly

With pedal

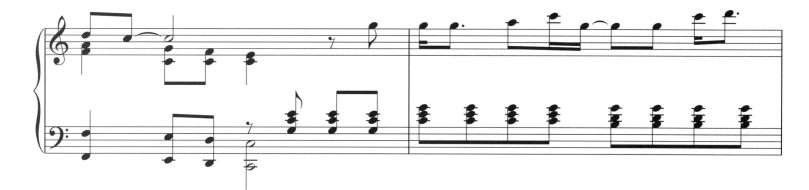

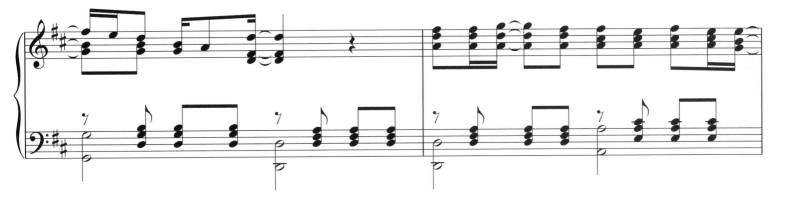

LUCY IN THE SKY WITH DIAMONDS

Words and Music by JOHN LENNON
and PAUL McCARTNEY

Moderately

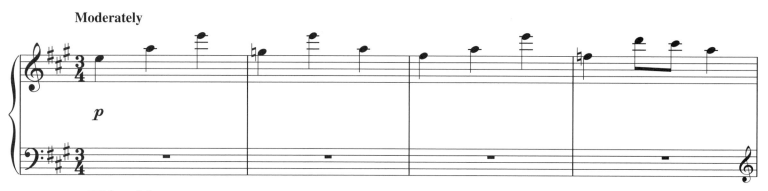

p

With pedal

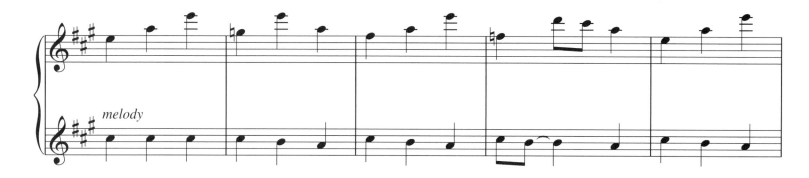

melody

melody

To Coda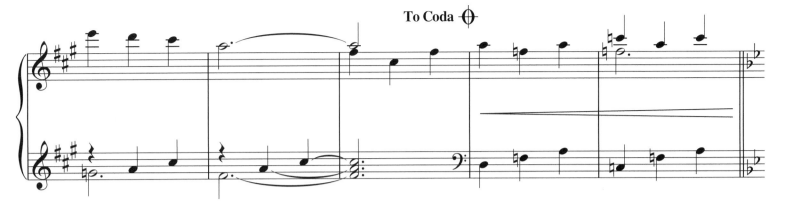

Tempo I

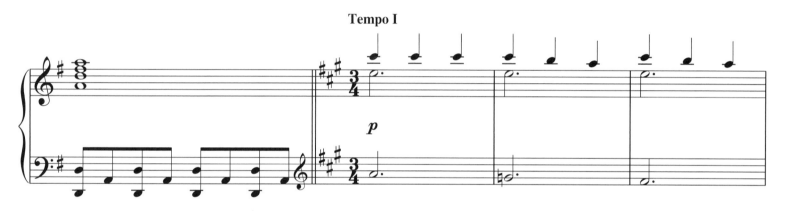

D.S. al Coda

CODA

Steady

MICHELLE

Words and Music by JOHN LENNON
and PAUL McCARTNEY

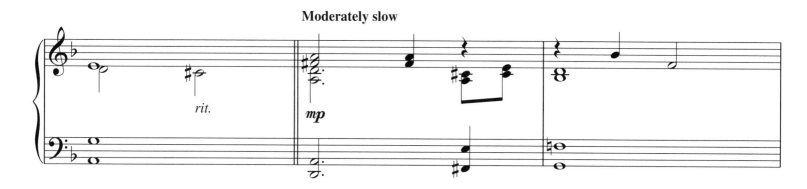

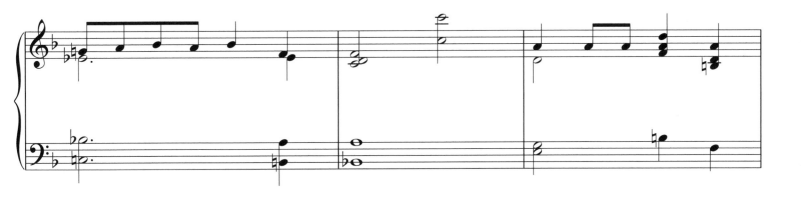

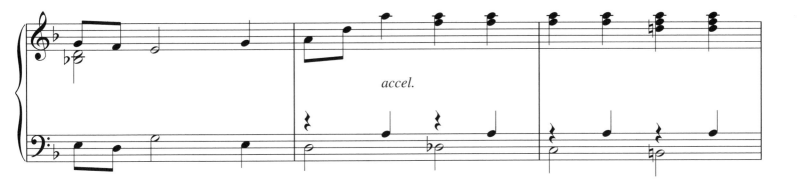

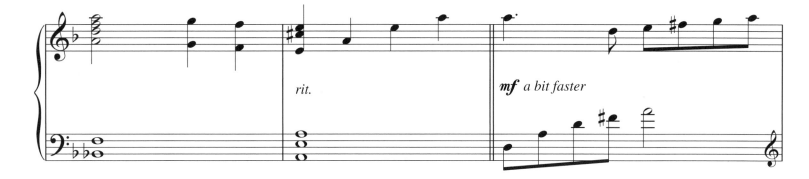

rit.

mf *a bit faster*

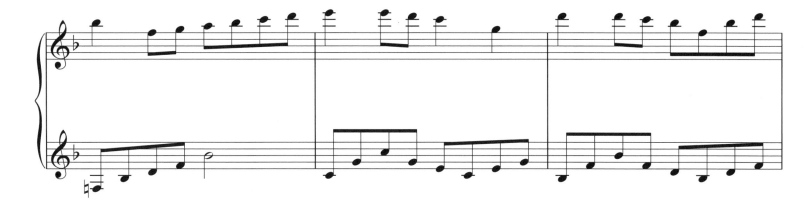

rit.

a tempo

71

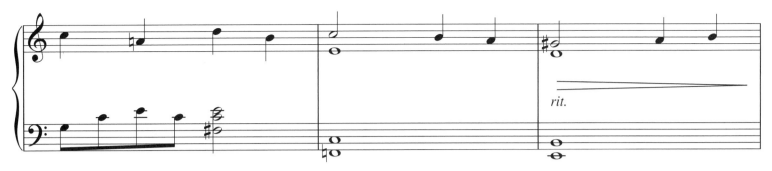

WHEN I'M SIXTY-FOUR

Words and Music by JOHN LENNON
and PAUL McCARTNEY

YELLOW SUBMARINE

Words and Music by JOHN LENNON
and PAUL McCARTNEY

March tempo

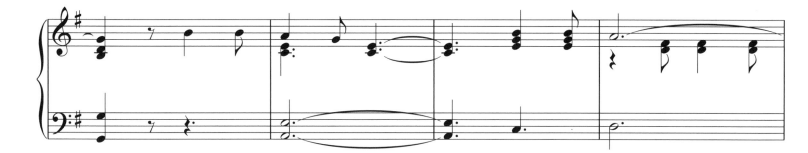

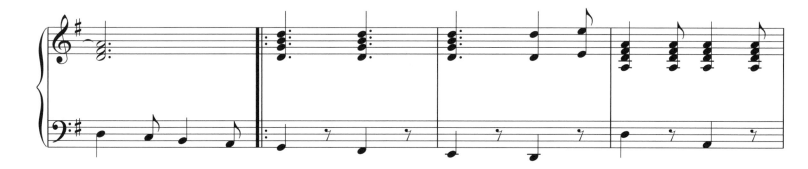

YESTERDAY

Words and Music by JOHN LENNON
and PAUL McCARTNEY

Moderately

THE LONG AND WINDING ROAD

Words and Music by JOHN LENNON
and PAUL McCARTNEY

Slowly

With pedal

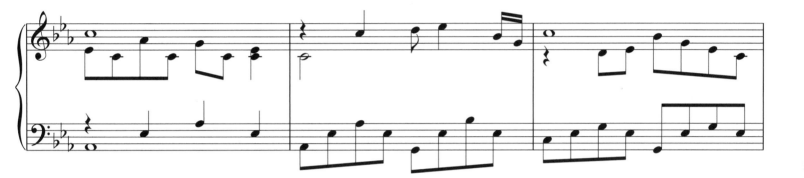

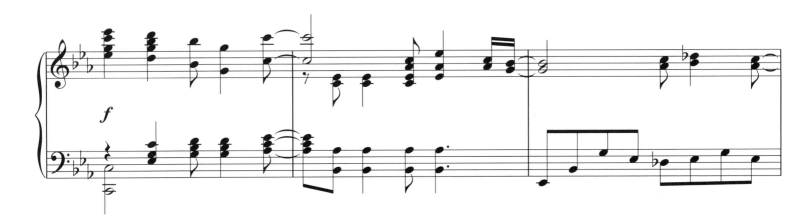